LIFE CYCLE OF A...

Broad Bean

Revised and Updated

Angela Royston

Heinemann
LIBRARY

www.heinemannlibrary.co.uk
Visit our website to find out more information about Heinemann Library books.

To order:
☎ Phone +44 (0) 1865 888066
🖷 Fax +44 (0) 1865 314091
🖥 Visit www.heinemannlibrary.co.uk

Heinemann Library is an imprint of Capstone Global Library Limited, a company incorporated in England and Wales having its registered office at 7 Pilgrim Street, London, EC4V 6LB - Registered company number: 6695582

"Heinemann" is a registered trademark of Pearson Education Limited, under licence to Capstone Global Library Limited

Text © Capstone Global Library Limited 1998, 2009
Second edition first published in hardback and paperback in 2009
The moral rights of the proprietor have been asserted.

Edited by Adrian Vigliano, Harriet Milles, and Diyan Leake
Designed by Kimberly R. Miracle and Tony Miracle
Original illustrations © Capstone Global Library Limited 1998, 2009
Illustrated by Alan Fraser
Picture research by Tracy Cummins and Heather Mauldin
Originated by Chroma Graphics (Overseas) Pte Ltd
Printed in China by South China Printing Company Ltd

ISBN 978 0 431 99943 2 (hardback)
13 12 11 10 09
10 9 8 7 6 5 4 3 2 1

ISBN 978 0 431 99961 6 (paperback)
13 12 11 10 09
10 9 8 7 6 5 4 3 2 1

British Library Cataloguing in Publication Data
Royston, Angela.
  Life cycle of a broad bean. -- 2nd ed.
  1. Fava bean--Life cycles--Juvenile literature.
  I. Title II. Broad bean
  571.8'2374-dc22

Acknowledgements
We would like to thank the following for permission to reproduce photographs: Alamy pp. 11 (© Helene Rogers), 12 (© Carl Newman); Getty Images 4 (© Images Of Africa); © Harry Smith Collection pp. 14, 20, 22, 25, 29 top right; © Heather Angel p. 13; Heinemann Raintree pp. 15 (© Trevor Clifford p. 17 (© Chris Honeywell), 18 (© Chris Honeywell); istockphoto pp. 10 (© Sabrina dei Nobili), 19 (© David T. Gomez), 21 (© Nigel Paul Monckton), 29 top left (© Sabrina dei Nobili), 29 (© David T. Gomez); Jupiter Images pp. 8 (© Oxford Scientific), 9 (© Oxford Scientific), 28 bottom (© Oxford Scientific); Nature Picture Library p. 6 (© Adam White); Photolibrary pp. 7 (© Oxford Scientific), 23 (© Oxford Scientific), 24 (© George Coppock), 26 (© Corbis), 28 top right (© Oxford Scientific); Shutterstock pp. 5 (© S. Fierros), 27 (© Philip Lange), 28 top left (© S. Fierros); Visuals Unlimited p. 16 (© Gap Photo/Tim Gainey).

Cover photograph reproduced with permission of © Gourmet Images.

We would like to thank Michael Bright for his invaluable help in the preparation of this book.

Every effort has been made to contact copyright holders of material reproduced in this book. Any omissions will be rectified in subsequent printings if notice is given to the publisher.

Contents

What is a bean? 4

1–7 days 6

2–3 weeks 8

3–10 weeks 10

11 weeks 12

12 weeks 14

12–14 weeks 18

14 weeks 20

20 weeks 22

20–24 weeks 24

A field of beans 26

Life cycle 28

Fact file 30

Glossary 31

More books to read 32

Index 32

Some words are shown in bold, **like this**. You can find out what they mean by looking in the glossary.

What is a bean?

Beans come in many shapes, sizes, and colours.

A bean is a **seed** that grows in a **pod**. We eat many kinds of beans, including black-eyed beans, red kidney beans, and broad beans.

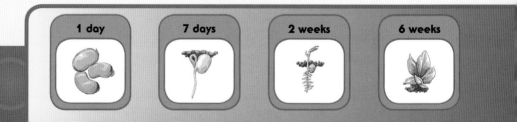

| 1 day | 7 days | 2 weeks | 6 weeks |

pod

The beans grow inside the pods.

This book shows what happens to a broad bean that is planted in spring.

12 weeks

14 weeks

20 weeks

The bean **seed** is planted in the **soil** with other bean seeds. The soil is watered and the beans begin to grow.

Bean seeds get pushed into the soil.

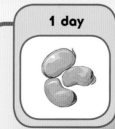

| 1 day | 7 days | 2 weeks | 6 weeks |

A **root** grows first. It pushes through the bean seed and grows down into the soil. It grows longer and longer.

The root grows down from the bean seed.

root

2–3 weeks

shoot

Now a shoot starts to grow. The bent **stem** pushes up through the **soil**. There are tiny leaves at the top of the stem.

The shoot grows up from the bean seed.

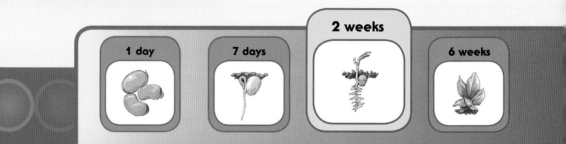

1 day

7 days

2 weeks

6 weeks

The shoot pushes right through the soil. The stem straightens and the leaves begin to open. More **roots** are growing.

Leaves grow and start to open at the end of the stem.

12 weeks

14 weeks

20 weeks

The leaves help the plant to bring in the things it needs to grow.

The leaves open out and turn dark green in the light. The leaves use sunlight, air, and water to make food for the plant.

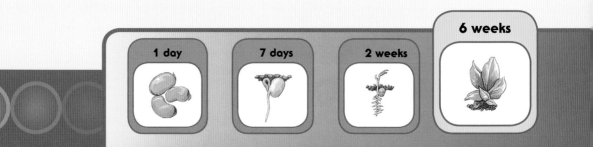

1 day

7 days

2 weeks

6 weeks

Flower buds form on the plants after about 10 weeks.

Water from the **soil** passes through the **roots** and up the **stem** to the leaves. The plant grows quickly. Flower buds begin to form.

12 weeks

14 weeks

20 weeks

11 weeks

A blackfly has laid its eggs under some of the leaves. Young blackflies have come out of the eggs. They are eating the leaves of the broad bean plant.

Blackflies can damage the leaves. This keeps the plant from growing.

1 day	7 days	2 weeks	6 weeks

A ladybird can eat
75 blackflies in one day!

If the plant becomes too damaged, it will die. Ladybirds eat lots of blackflies. This helps to save the plant.

12 weeks

14 weeks

20 weeks

12 weeks

A bean plant has many flowers.

Thick groups of flowers open at the bottom of the leaves. The flowers are black and white.

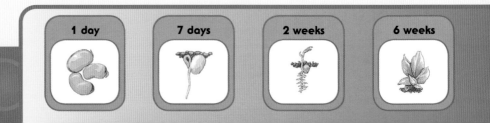

1 day	7 days	2 weeks	6 weeks

There are tiny grains of **pollen** and a sweet juice called **nectar** in each flower. Insects come to drink the nectar.

The pollen and nectar are at the centre of the flower.

12 weeks

14 weeks

20 weeks

pollen

This bee is sucking up nectar from a broad bean plant flower.

A bee crawls right into the flower. As it sips the **nectar**, grains of **pollen** collect on its hairy legs.

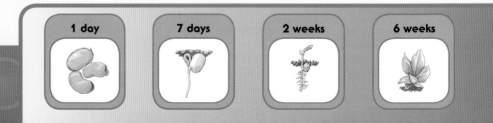

| 1 day | 7 days | 2 weeks | 6 weeks |

This insect helps move pollen from one flower to another.

Some of the pollen from another flower rubs off inside this one. This makes **seeds** form inside the flower.

12 weeks

14 weeks

20 weeks

12–14 weeks

Bean pods form as the flowers die.

When a **seed** inside the **pod** joins with a grain of **pollen** from another flower, it becomes a new bean. The flower dies and the beans swell.

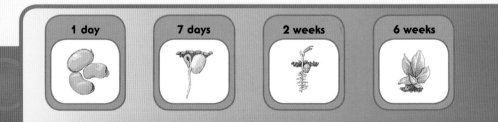

| 1 day | 7 days | 2 weeks | 6 weeks |

The beans are protected inside the tough, thick pod. As the beans grow, the pod grows longer and heavier.

Many heavy bean pods can hang from one plant.

12 weeks

14 weeks

20 weeks

14 weeks

Each plant has lots of **pods**. Sometimes the pods are so heavy that they make the **stem** bend down.

Look how many pods are growing on this plant!

1 day	7 days	2 weeks	6 weeks

Most broad bean pods have 3–8 beans in them.

stalk

The inside of the pod is soft and wet. Each bean is joined to the pod by a short stalk. The stalk brings food and water to the bean.

12 weeks

14 weeks

20 weeks

20 weeks

When the beans are fully grown, the **pod** begins to turn black. The plant has done its job and its leaves begin to die.

The bean plant starts to die when the bean pods are fully grown.

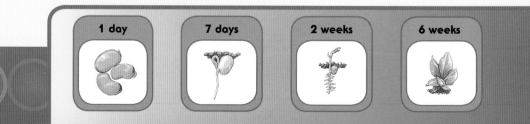

| 1 day | 7 days | 2 weeks | 6 weeks |

This hungry field mouse is eating the beans that are on the ground.

Some of the pods fall to the ground and split open. Field mice like to eat beans. They eat the beans when a pod splits open.

12 weeks

14 weeks

20 weeks

Bean pods can be picked by hand or by machine.

Most beans are picked before they are fully grown. They are more juicy to eat then. In autumn the whole plant withers and dies.

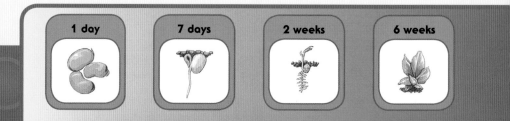

1 day

7 days

2 weeks

6 weeks

Some dried bean seeds are saved to be planted the next year.

Not all of the beans are eaten. As they dry, they turn hard and brown. These new **seeds** will be planted next spring to grow into new plants.

12 weeks

14 weeks

20 weeks

A field of beans

The broad beans are planted in rows.

Farmers plant beans in huge fields. The **pods** are picked and most are sent to factories to be frozen or put in tins.

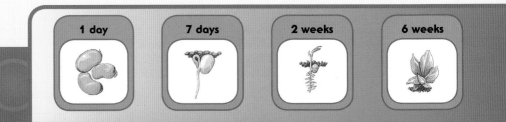

| 1 day | 7 days | 2 weeks | 6 weeks |

This tractor is chopping up dead plants and covering them with soil.

The plants will be cut up and covered with **soil**. As the plants rot, they slowly break up and become part of the soil.

12 weeks   14 weeks   20 weeks

Life cycle

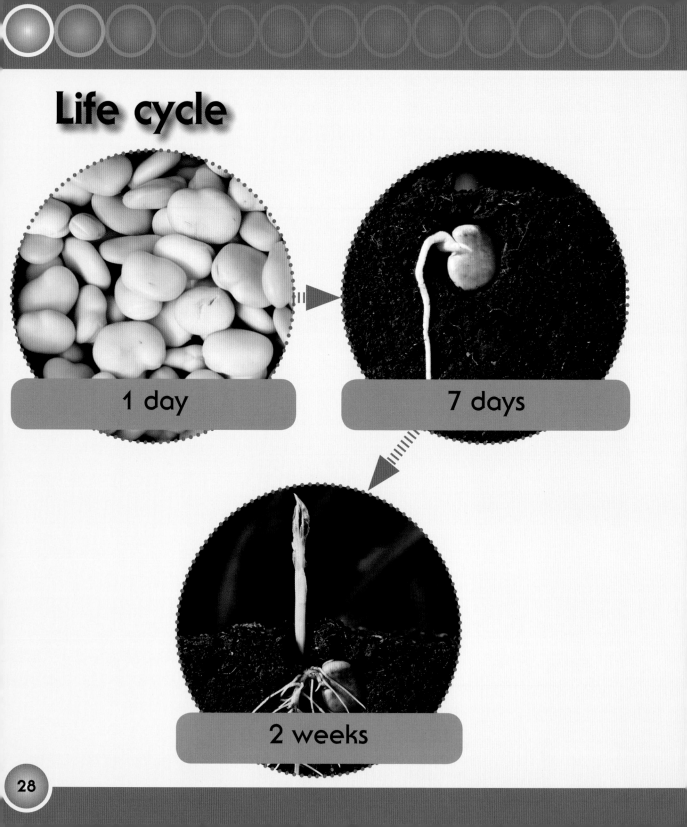

1 day

7 days

2 weeks

6 weeks

12 weeks

14 weeks

Fact file

 In just four months a broad bean grows from a seed to a plant as tall as an adult person.

 The bean that Jack planted in *Jack and the Beanstalk* was a broad bean.

 One broad bean plant can produce over 300 beans.

 In Ancient Greece and Rome, rich people would not eat beans because they thought they would damage their sight.

Glossary

nectar a sweet, sugary juice in the centre of a flower

pod tough, thick shell that holds beans or other seeds

pollen fine yellow dust made in the centre of a flower

root part of a plant under the ground which takes in water from the soil

seed part of a plant that can grow into a new plant

soil top layer of the ground, where plants grow

stem stalk that supports the leaves, flowers, and fruit of a plant

More books to read

From Bean to Bean Plant, Anita Ganeri (Heinemann Library, 2006)

How Do Plants Grow? (World of Plants), Louise and Richard Spilsbury (Heinemann Library, 2006)

The Life of a Broad Bean, Clare Hibbert (Raintree, 2004)

Index

bees 16
blackflies 12, 13
field mice 23
flowers 11, 13, 14, 15, 16, 17, 18
food 10, 21
insects 15, 17
ladybirds 13
leaves 8, 9, 10, 11, 12, 13, 22
nectar 15, 16
plants 10, 11, 12, 13, 14, 16, 19, 20, 22, 24, 25, 27, 30

pods 4, 5, 18, 19, 20, 21, 22, 23, 24, 26
pollen 15, 16, 17, 18
roots 7, 9, 11
seeds 4, 6, 7, 8, 17, 18, 25, 30
shoots 8, 9
soil 6, 7, 8, 9, 11, 27
stalks 21
stems 8, 9, 11, 20
water 10, 11, 21